MW01164939

MARY
WOLLSTONECRAFT

Kitty Warnock

Hamish Hamilton
London

Mrs Mary Wollstonecroft

IN HER OWN TIME

This series focuses a spotlight on women whose lives and work have all too often been overlooked yet who have made significant contributions to society in many different areas: from politics and painting to science and social reform.

Women's voices have in the past been the silent ones of history. In Britain, for example, the restrictions of society, the time-consuming nature of domestic work, and the poor educational opportunities available to women until this century, have meant that not only did women rarely have the opportunity to explore their abilities beyond those which society expected of them, but also that their aspirations and achievements were often not recorded.

This series profiles a number of women who, through a combination of character and circumstance, were able to influence ideas and attitudes or contribute to the arts and sciences. None of them were alone in their ambitions. There must have been many other women whose experiences we know nothing of because they were not recorded. Many of the 'ordinary' women who have supported the so-called 'exceptional' women of history also displayed great courage, skill and determination. Political and social change, in particular, has been accelerated by the pioneering work of individual women but rarely achieved without the collective efforts of masses of unknown women.

The work of many women in the series took them into the public eye: some were honoured and celebrated, more frequently they faced disapproval or lack of sympathy with their ideas. Many were ahead of their time and only later did their pioneering activities gain public respect. Others found their lives so deeply entangled with current events that their path was virtually chosen for them. A few were not closely involved with contemporary society but highly original characters who nevertheless influenced or informed others. By exploring the struggles, hopes, failures and achievements of these women, we can discover much about the society they lived in and how each made their personal contribution — in their own way, in their own time.

Olivia Bennett

HAMISH HAMILTON CHILDREN'S BOOKS
Published by the Penguin Group
27 Wrights Lane, London W8 5TZ, England
Viking Penguin Inc., 40 West 23rd Street, New York, New York 10010, U.S.A.
Penguin Books Australia Ltd, Ringwood, Victoria, Australia
Penguin Books Canada Ltd, 2801 John Street, Markham, Ontario, Canada L3R 1B4
Penguin Books (N.Z.) Ltd, 182–190 Wairau Road, Auckland 10, New Zealand

Penguin Books Ltd, Registered Offices: Harmondsworth, Middlesex, England

First published in Great Britain 1988 by
Hamish Hamilton Children's Books
Copyright © 1988 by Kitty Warnock

Design by Sally Boothroyd
Cover design by Clare Truscott

British Library Cataloguing in Publication Data
Warnock, Kitty
Mary Wollstonecraft.—(In her own time).
1. Shelley, Mary Wollstonecraft—Biography
—Juvenile literature   2. Novelists,
English—18th century—Biography—
Juvenile literature
1. Title   II. Series
823'.7   PR5398
ISBN 0-241-12151-5

Typeset in Palatino by Katerprint Typesetting Services
Printed in Great Britain by
Butler & Tanner Ltd, Frome, Somerset

Contents

Chapter One

The First Feminist

Portrait of Mary Wollstonecraft. Mary may not have been quite so pretty and gentle as she appears here. Portrait-painters often made their sitters look more beautiful than they actually were. Mary herself thought that looks were unimportant and spoke out fiercely against the way her society valued a woman's appearance more than her mind or personality.

Almost exactly two hundred years ago, in 1792, a book was published in Britain which argued that women should have the same rights as men to education, employment, and the vote. Today, these ideas are widely accepted, but at the time they caused a sensation.

The author was Mary Wollstonecraft. She was thirty-two when she wrote the book. Mary knew that her ideas were unusual for her time, but she could hardly have predicted how long it was to be before people were ready to accept her suggestions and put them into practice.

It would be 136 years before women gained the vote on equal terms with men. University education did not become available to women until 1869, with the establishment of Girton College, Cambridge; and although London University accepted women in 1878, it was not until 1948 that women could become full members of Cambridge University. Elizabeth Garrett Anderson, the first woman to obtain a licence to practise as a doctor in Britain, did so in 1865. Right up to the Second World War, married women were not allowed to work in the Civil Service. And it was not until the 1970s that laws were passed making it illegal to pay a woman less for doing the same job as a man, or to refuse a woman a job just because of her sex.

Mary Wollstonecraft was a woman of action as well as words. Despite the lack of opportunities for women, she tried to put her

ideas into practice in her own life, and
suffered for doing so. She wanted to fulfil
herself as a whole person – as a thinker, a
worker, a lover, and a mother. She was
determined to prove that a whole woman is
just as good as a whole man. Above all, Mary
tried to be free. She wanted to work, and
think, and love as she chose to, without
being tied to a husband or anyone else. This
was difficult in an age when middle-class
women were expected to be content with a
narrow life at home as a wife and mother. In
fact, most people thought women were not
capable of doing anything else. They thought
women's abilities and intelligence were less
than men's.

A minority of people agreed with Mary's
ideas in theory; but the majority were deeply
shocked by her behaviour. They could not
accept a woman rejecting marriage and
having an illegitimate child as she did. This
disapproval lasted long after Mary's death,
and cast a shadow over the way people
responded to her ideas for many years.

Yet Mary had understood some important
truths about how society tried to keep
women in second place. Nobody before her
or for a long time afterwards explained
women's position so well. Mary is often
called 'the first feminist'.

Chapter Two

Childhood

Mary was born on 27 April 1759, in
Spitalfields in London's East End. Spitalfields
was a cloth-making area. Most of the people
there were weavers, who spent their days
crowded into small dark rooms working at
their clattering looms, struggling to earn
enough money to stay alive. Mary's family

*Christ Church in Spitalfields,
London. Mary was born nearby,
and the street her family lived in
may have been very like this.*

lived in a small house in an ordinary street, but they were not as poor as their neighbours. Mary's grandfather had established a successful weaving business, and was quite well-off. But Mary's father was lazy and a hopeless business man, and he never made any money.

Mary's parents were not happy in Spitalfields. They felt that, with the money Mary's grandfather had made, they ought to be enjoying the comfortable life of the upper classes. So they moved to a farm in Epping and then to one in Barking, just outside London. Here Mary's father tried to live as a gentleman farmer and make friends with his upper-class neighbours, the local landowners. But he wasn't a good farmer. He wasted his money on drink and sport, and soon had to sell his farm and move away. All through Mary's childhood the family moved from place to place – to Yorkshire, to London again, to Wales, and then back to London. Mary never had the chance to settle down and feel she belonged in one place.

She liked the country much more than London. She liked to run about in the garden by herself, and she loved animals. For she was not happy at home. She had a brother Ned, two years older than she was, and two more brothers and two sisters, all younger. Her parents and grandfather gave most of their love and attention to Ned. Mary felt this was unfair. Did he deserve more than she did, just because he was a boy?

Being a girl

As she grew up, Mary learnt that girls in her social class were treated differently from boys in many ways. Boys were allowed to run around playing noisy and energetic games,

[Men] should be active and strong, [women] passive and weak; it is necessary the one should have both the power and the will, and that the other should make little resistance . . .

Jean-Jacques Rousseau (1712–1778) in Emile, 1762.

while girls were told to sit quietly indoors. Boys were encouraged to have strong personalities and to try to get what they wanted. Girls were supposed to think of others all the time, and to want nothing for themselves. Boys were allowed to tell other people what to do, girls always had to do what they were told.

All this was because society was organised around the belief that men and women were created to fulfil different functions in life. Many people thought that the role of men was to rule and to control the worlds of politics, business and the arts, while women

Page from a children's book showing some of the games children played in Mary's time. It is significant that there are three pictures of boys, and in all three they are playing outside, while the single picture of girls shows them playing indoors. Notice the girls' clothes, too — they tell you a lot about how girls were expected to behave.

11

were homemakers, companions and comforters – whose role was to have children and look after the world within the home.

This was justified by the idea that men's and women's characters were different. People thought men were the stronger sex, in body and in mind. They were able to lead, and make difficult decisions. Women on the other hand were considered gentle, fragile and less able – in spite of the fact that working-class women were working alongside men in coal mining and other heavy jobs. The responsibilities of middle-class women were limited to their homes and families, and they were expected to let their husbands tell them what to do.

Because of these ideas, middle-class women were taught to behave in certain ways. As they were brought up in the understanding that they needed men to look after them, they had to make sure men wanted to do this; so they had to think all the time of how to keep men happy. Women had to be flattering, respectful, and attractive. And since the theory was that they didn't need to know how to do anything outside the house, education for girls was thought unnecessary. Indeed, most people thought that it would be a waste of time, as they believed women were not capable of learning and thinking the way men were. Many people were influenced by the French philosopher and writer Jean Jacques Rousseau, who had described the 'ideal woman' as 'passive and weak' in his popular book *Emile, or Education*.

Even as a child, Mary rejected these ideas. She did not believe that girls were inferior to boys. Long before she was able to read Rousseau's book for herself, she decided that girls' minds were just as good as boys', or

T H E
H I S T O R
O F
Little GOODY TWO-SHOES ;
Otherwise called,
Mrs. MARGERY TWO-SHOES.
W I T H
The Means by which she acquired her
Learning and Wisdom, and in conse-
quence thereof her Estate ; set forth
at large for the Benefit of those,

Who from a State of Rags and Care,
And having Shoes but half a Pair ;
Their Fortune and their Fame would fix,
And gallop in a Coach and Six.

See the Original Manuscript in the *Vatican*
at *Rome*, and the Cuts by *Michael Angelo.*
Illustrated with the Comments of our
great modern Critics.

L O N D O N :
Printed for J. NEWBERY, at the *Bible* and
Sun in St. *Paul's Church-yard*, 1765.
[Price Six Pence.]

Little Goody Two-Shoes

would be, at least, if they had the same education. She herself had a strong will, too, and a strong temper, and she refused to hide them.

Her parents tried to teach her to be a 'good girl', but with little success. As far as Mary could see, being the kind of 'good girl' her parents wanted meant being weak and stupid and thinking about nothing except clothes and how to make herself pretty. Mary didn't think prettiness was important. For her, knowledge and ideas were far more valuable than beauty.

Little Goody Two-shoes was the first novel published in England especially for children. It tells the 'improving' story of a poor orphan who works hard to educate herself and becomes a travelling teacher. The book was published in 1765, and was popular for the next hundred years or more.

'Black Monday, or The
Departure for School'
This picture, printed in 1790,
reflects what was common in
middle-class families at the time
— it is a son who is going away
to school, not a daughter.

Her parents wanted Ned to go to university and become a lawyer, but they didn't bother about their daughters' education. It seems to have been the family's housekeeper who taught Mary to read. Fortunately, when the family was living in Beverley, Yorkshire, there happened to be a girls' school nearby, and Mary was allowed to attend it.

Growing up

By the time she reached adolescence, Mary knew there were two things she wanted from life – one was the freedom to think for herself, the other was a special kind of personal relationship. She wanted an intense relationship in which the two friends would be equal but completely committed and devoted to one another. She must have been a difficult friend to have. She got jealous easily, and often quarrelled with her friends when she thought they did not love her enough. In a letter to her friend Jane, when she was fourteen, Mary said,

'I have a heart that scorns disguise . . . I have formed romantic notions of friendship . . . I am a little singular in my ideas of love and friendship; I must have the first place or none.'

Both these things Mary wanted, intellectual freedom and complete emotional commitment, are difficult to achieve at any time. But they were especially difficult then, because women had so little freedom and power in society. Mary's life was bound to be hard as she tried to fulfil her ambitions.

'A Village School'
This picture illustrates the low opinion most people had of schools in Mary's time. The master is brutal, the boys are wild, and nobody seems to be learning anything.

First Jobs

By the time she was eighteen, Mary was desperate to leave home. But how could she do it? It was unheard of for a girl to live by herself. Girls were supposed to stay at home and wait for a husband. But Mary was determined that she would never marry. What she had seen of her parents' relationship had put her off the idea. Her

'A Man Trap'
This cartoon of 1780 makes fun of women who think of nothing but fashion, flirtations and social life. (Notice the invitation cards in the rack behind her!) It was probably painted by a man. What he did not show was that if women were like this, it was because society encouraged them to be so — something Mary pointed out many times in her writings.

father was selfish, violent and irresponsible. Her mother wept and complained but was powerless to change anything.

Mary thought that it was not just her parents' marriage, but all marriages, that were like this. All the people she knew were middle-class like herself, and to Mary it seemed that the middle-class woman was like her husband's servant: she had to care for him, entertain him, and obey him, however badly he treated her. He 'paid' her by giving her food, clothes, and a house to live in, but she never had any money of her own, so she was totally dependent on him. And she was not free to leave. According to the law at that time, a married woman had no legal existence apart from her husband, and no right to own property herself. She could hardly survive without him. Not surprisingly, most women did accept marriage, with all its drawbacks. They had little choice.

Rich women, it is true, did not have to work like servants. They employed people to do their housework and look after their children. But all the same they suffered a servant's lack of freedom. They were just supposed to sit at home. They weren't encouraged to use their minds to do any useful or challenging work. Hardly surprisingly, many became very bored – and boring, since they had little to occupy them but idle gossip and domestic details.

Jobs for women

For working-class women it was different; they had to work, to help their families stay alive. In the country they worked on farms, in towns they worked in shops or crowded workshops. The Industrial Revolution was under way, and more and more women had

[Wives are] confined in cages like a feathered race, they have nothing to do but plume themselves and stalk with mock majesty from perch to perch. It is true that they are provided with food and raiment, for which they neither toil nor spin; but health, liberty and virtue are given in exchange.

Mary Wollstonecraft in
A Vindication of the Rights of Woman.

jobs in mills and factories. The largest number, especially of unmarried women, were servants, for not only the rich but also farmers and tradesmen had maids to do the household work.

Most of these jobs involved long hours of hard physical work for low pay. Conditions were bad. No middle-class woman would do this kind of job. In fact, there were very few jobs thought suitable for a middle-class girl like Mary. Professions such as medicine and law were closed to women. Mary envied Ned, who was setting up as a lawyer, but she could not train for any similar career herself.

If Mary did not want to get married, what else could she do? What alternatives were there for middle-class women who wanted to be independent, or who had no husband or relatives to support them? Virtually the only

'Morning employments',
1789. Embroidery, music,
children, pets, perhaps visiting
some friends — these domestic
interests were supposed to keep
middle-class women happy, but
they were not enough for Mary.

option was to become a teacher, either in a school or as a governess in a rich home. Mary did not particularly like children. There was one other possibility to consider. Women were not supposed to live alone, so sometimes unmarried women and widows, if they could afford it, employed another single woman to live with them. This was the job Mary chose. Defying her parents' disapproval, she left home and went to Bath as the paid companion of a rich widow, Mrs Dawson.

Mary's job was to chat or read to Mrs Dawson when she was bored, to escort her and carry her bags and shawls when she went out, and to help her with little tasks like writing letters. Mary was more than a servant to her employer, but a lot less than a friend. It was humiliating work, living at the beck and call of this bad-tempered old lady, but Mary stuck it out for three years. At least she was meeting new people, and seeing something of the world. She had escaped from her family. She dreamed of earning enough money to set up home with her beloved friend Fanny Blood.

Then Mary's mother fell ill, and Mary was asked to come home and nurse her. A few months later she died. The family broke up. Mary's father went to Wales again. He soon remarried, and didn't take much further interest in his children. Ned didn't want to look after all three of his sisters, so Mary was invited to live with the family of her friend Fanny.

Life with the Bloods

She spent a miserable eighteen months with the Bloods. The family was rather like Mary's own. Mr Blood was selfish and violent, even

[A companion is] Above the servants, yet considered by them as a spy, and ever reminded of her inferiority when in conversation with superiors . . . Should any of the visitors take notice of her, and she for a moment forget her subordinate state, she is sure to be reminded of it.

Mary Wollstonecraft in Thoughts on the Education of Daughters, *1786.*

Cartoonist Thomas Rowlandson's view of 'The Comforts of Bath'. Bath, where Mary lived when she was working as a companion, was for many years a fashionable holiday resort. It was also a favourite place for the sick and elderly to retire to or visit for a 'cure'. Drinking water from its mineral springs was thought to be good for the health. Most of the people in this picture seem to be suffering from over-indulgence in food and wine!

worse than her own father, and his wife was weak and helpless. Mr Blood did not earn enough to support his family, so his wife and daughters had to find work. The only work they could do was sewing, at home. Mary joined in, though she hated needlework. She felt more and more angry that there were so few jobs for women. It seemed to her that women would only be able to build their own independent lives and stand up to their husbands if they were able to earn money for themselves.

Fanny Blood could see only one way of escaping from her miserable home: she would marry a man who was richer and kinder than her own family. But what happened to Fanny confirmed Mary's view that marriage was a trap for women. For after Fanny fell in love and got engaged, her fiancé went away to Portugal on business. It was several years before he asked her to join him. All Fanny could do was stay at home and wait. Mary was sorry for her, but angry with her, too. She felt Fanny should have known that in marriage it was always the man who did what he wanted, never the woman.

To make matters worse, Fanny was ill. Like so many people at that time, she had tuberculosis, a lung disease. There was no treatment for it, and they all knew that she was probably dying.

'Gin Lane' by satirist William Hogarth, 1751. His point is that poor people turned to gin, which was cheap, as a way of forgetting about their troubles. Consequently they neglected their children, work and homes and made their situation much worse. Hogarth's picture is an exaggeration, but Mary knew that scenes of misery and desperation nearly as bad as this were common in poor parts of London.

Eliza's marriage

The hopeless period with the Bloods ended dramatically. Mary did something which broke society's rules and shocked everyone, including her family. It was in her character to do what she believed was right, however much other people disapproved, however difficult it was.

Mary's sister Eliza had married a man she loved. A year later, after she'd had a baby, she was depressed and had a nervous breakdown. Her husband asked Mary to come and help look after Eliza and the baby. As soon as she arrived, Mary decided that Eliza's husband was treating her badly. The only solution she could see was for Eliza to leave him. Mary was a much stronger personality than Eliza. She persuaded her to run away, leaving her baby daughter behind.

In those days, for a woman to leave her husband was a rare and shocking event. Mary and Eliza had to go into hiding so that Eliza's husband and Ned couldn't find them. They rented rooms using false names. Mary didn't want any help or interference from men. She wanted to prove that women could manage on their own.

Unfortunately the brave adventure turned out badly. Eliza was miserable without her baby (who died before she was a year old). She began to wish that she had never run away. Although Eliza was so unhappy, Mary wouldn't give up and let men take over again. She was determined that she and Eliza and Fanny should set up home together and support themselves. But all three of them were exhausted by the strain of the past six months. Illness and a long cold winter made things worse, and they hardly had any money. How were they going to manage?

I knew I should be . . . the 'shameful incendiary' in this shocking affair of a woman leaving her bed-fellow . . . In short, 'tis contrary to all the rules of conduct that are published for the benefit of new married Ladies . . .

Mary Wollstonecraft, in a letter to her sister Everina

Chapter Four

Mary's School

Faced with the problem of how to support herself and the others, Mary decided to open a school. She borrowed money and rented a house in Newington Green, which was then a village on the north-east edge of London. She moved into it with her two sisters and Fanny, and advertised that they were starting a school. It was a popular area for schools – there were several in nearby Hackney – so Mary thought it would be easy to get pupils.

In Mary's day, there were no state schools. Education was a privilege, not a right. Parents who wanted their children to be educated had to pay for them to have private lessons at home or go to private schools.

Newington Green on the edge of London, where Mary ran a school. Many religious dissenters with radical political ideas lived here. Mary made life-long friends among them, and they probably changed the course of her life.

Working-class children usually received little or no education. They had to start working very young to earn extra money for their families. There were some schools run by local churches or by religious charities which they could attend, but their parents could not often afford to lose their labour for long. The majority of the population did not learn how to read and write properly.

'A Young Ladies' Boarding School', about 1770.
This was the kind of school where middle-class girls were taught nothing much except how to be 'lady-like'. The time-table seems to be made up of dancing, music and singing, and embroidery. Mary's sisters attended a school in Putney rather like this one, but in her own school Mary would have tried to teach more serious subjects.

Education for girls

During the eighteenth century more people were recognising the importance of education, and there was a lot of interest in it. This era is sometimes called the Age of Reason, or Enlightenment. Many intellectuals of the time argued that if only people were educated, they would naturally behave in a considerate and sensible way, and a just and caring society would be the result. There was an optimism about such ideas and much discussion took place. What kind of learning was best? What should the aim of education be? One of the most controversial questions was, what should girls learn? Rousseau's ideas had a lot of influence. He believed education was very important – for boys. Girls only needed to learn how to be good wives.

Most people agreed, as we have seen, that girls were less intelligent than boys. And of course, as women were rarely encouraged to use their minds, they must often have seemed quite foolish. One complained, 'We (women) are permitted no books but such as tend to the weakening . . . of the mind . . . it is looked upon as in a degree criminal to improve our reason, or fancy we have any.'

Not everybody accepted the idea that women were less intelligent than men. A few believed, as Mary did, that girls had the same abilities as boys. It was education they lacked, not intelligence. The writer of the complaint above, Mary Wortley Montagu, was one of the exceptional women who was lucky enough to be educated at home and succeeded in developing her mind. She became famous as a writer of political essays and letters. Women like her and a few others had proved that women could be just as

It follows that woman is expressly formed to please the man . . . This . . . is one of the laws of nature. If woman be formed to please and be subjected to man, it is her place, doubtless, to render herself agreeable to him, instead of challenging his passion.

Jean-Jacques Rousseau (1712–1778) in Emile, 1762.

I have often thought it as one of the most barbarous customs in the world, considering us a civilised and Christian country, that we deny the advantages of learning to women. We reproach the sex every day with folly and impertinence; while I am confident, had they advantages of education equal with us, they would be guilty of less than ourselves.

Daniel Defoe, Essay upon Projects, 1698

clever and creative as men. Such views were quite acceptable among a select group of the country's intellectuals, of whom the famous writer Samuel Johnson was one. He made the point that any man who did not believe in educating girls was frightened of being outstripped by his womenfolk. However, outside the small circle of the literary elite, any woman who showed intellectual ability was ridiculed and branded a 'bluestocking'.

Thus, in 1784 when Mary Wollstonecraft was opening her school, most people still agreed that a good education was wasted on girls. Even those who did send their daughters to school, did not care very much what they learned there. Teachers were badly paid and not respected – not surprisingly, in many cases, because they were often badly educated themselves so the standard of their teaching was very low. As Elizabeth Ham recorded, 'I used to go regularly to a Dame's school, where the learning I picked up very soon exceeded all that was possessed by old Molly Brown, the Mistress. Her instrument of authority was a long stick with which she could reach the head of any one of her pupils.'

The failure of Mary's school

Mary's school may have been better than most, but it was not a success, and didn't last long. She worked hard, but she didn't have the character to be a good teacher. She had little patience, and did not really understand people who were not as clever or as strong-willed as she was. Some pupils came, but they did not stay long.

There were domestic troubles too. The house Mary had rented was a big one, and she had to let some of the rooms out to lodgers, to make more money. But like the pupils, the lodgers left – sometimes without paying. Meanwhile, Fanny was becoming weaker and couldn't do much work. Soon she left to join her fiancé in Portugal. (She died in childbirth a year later. The strain of having a baby was too much for her sick body. Mary was with her at the time. She was grief-stricken at seeing her best friend die, but there was nothing she could do to help her.)

The school had to close down. But it had one good result, which changed Mary's life completely – it introduced her to some new people, her neighbours in Newington Green. Until now, Mary had met very few people she really respected and felt at home with. Now she found a whole group of friends, whom she liked and who liked her.

The Dissenters

Mary's new friends were a group of people known as 'Dissenters'. The name means that they dissented from, or disagreed with, the generally accepted ideas of the time. They were very serious people, but optimistic. They believed, as Mary did, that all people are equal and naturally good.

Most members of the upper classes did not share this view. They felt that the masses of ordinary people were unintelligent, idle and disorderly by nature, and must not be allowed to have any power – they were certainly not fit to vote and decide how the country should be governed. But the Dissenters disagreed. They believed that if and when people are irresponsible, it is ignorance and poverty that make them so. For all human beings have rational minds which they can use, given the chance, to make decisions for themselves and choose the

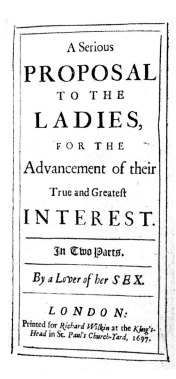

A Serious

PROPOSAL

TO THE

LADIES,

FOR THE

Advancement of their

True and Greatest

INTEREST.

In Two Parts.

By a Lover of her SEX.

LONDON:

Printed for *Richard Wilkin* at the *King's-Head* in St. *Paul's Church-Yard*, 1697.

Title page of A Serious Proposal to the Ladies, *first published by Mary Astell in 1694. Her proposal was to establish a college where women could go to escape for a while from family and social duties and devote themselves to studying, just like men did in universities. At the time, most people thought this idea was laughable.*

right course of action. If the wealth of the upper classes was shared among working people and everyone had the chance to be educated, then, the Dissenters felt, everyone would develop his or her better qualities.

They also believed everyone should be free to think what he or she liked and should have the vote. In other words, they were democrats. They wanted a new kind of life for people in Britain. They were sometimes called 'radicals', because their aim was a radical, or complete, change. What they wanted was a kind of revolution, although they hoped it would not be a violent one. The old political and economic system would be destroyed, and a new life could begin, with freedom, equality and a share of wealth for everyone.

Nowadays, the ideas of the Dissenters are quite acceptable. Our society is based on the idea that everyone has the right to education, and the right to vote for the kind of government he or she wants. It is increasingly accepted that many crimes are caused by poverty and bad working and living conditions. But in Mary's time, these ideas were unusual. And to put them into practice would have meant, of course, taking away power and wealth from the ruling classes. So these people, and many others who didn't want changes, disliked and feared the Dissenters.

Another reason for people's suspicion of Dissenters was that they did not belong to the Church of England. Because of this they were not allowed to attend universities or take jobs in government. They had their own chapels, schools and colleges, and their own bookshops. They stuck together, and made friends mostly with each other.

Mary found that her new friends shared many of her ideas. They agreed that the poverty of the majority of people in Britain was unjust and could be removed by social change. Some of the Dissenters, though not all, believed like her that men and women were equals. For the first time in her life, Mary found people who were not horrified by her ideas. She could talk with them about politics, literature, society and events of the time. She was respected and welcomed, and made many life-long friends.

Richard Price, a famous political philosopher and mathematician, was living in nearby Hackney when Mary came to Stoke Newington, and he befriended her and influenced her thinking. He was one of the many radicals who welcomed the French Revolution. When it began, he gave a sermon expressing his support.

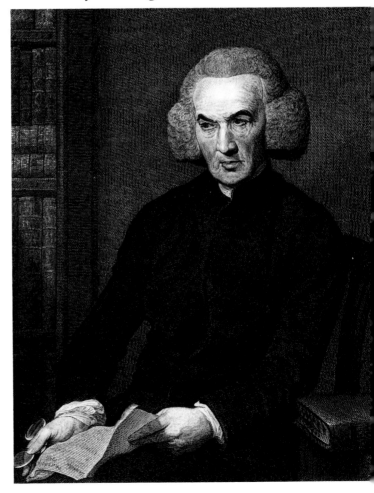

Chapter Five

Becoming a Writer

When her school closed after two years, Mary had to look around yet again for some way of earning a living and paying back her debts. Ned was quite prosperous now. He was a well-established lawyer, and besides, it was he who had inherited most of their grandfather's wealth. But he refused to help

Joseph Johnson

St Paul's Churchyard. Joseph Johnson's shop was in this street next to St Paul's Cathedral in London. Many radical writers and thinkers, including Mary, used to meet each other there and discuss their ideas and the affairs of the day.

Mary. He felt that her problems were all her own fault and she must suffer the consequences of her behaviour. If she had stayed quietly at home like other women, he thought, she could have made a good marriage and none of her troubles would have happened. He couldn't accept that for someone like her that kind of life was impossible.

Mary had a new idea. She might be able to earn some money by writing. She got in touch with a publisher called Joseph Johnson, who published many books by Dissenters. His bookshop near St Paul's Cathedral was one of their favourite meeting places. The room above the shop was often full of lively political and philosophical discussions. Joseph was especially interested in books about education. He decided that he and Mary could help each other. She could write educational books especially for women and children, which he was sure would sell well.

31

Books for women

Books for women and for children were quite a new idea, but there was a growing demand for them. More and more women, especially in the middle classes, were learning to read. Lending libraries had been established twenty years earlier, and they soon became popular. Then as now, women liked to relax with light romantic novels, and there were many magazines as well. Some were similar to women's magazines today. They had articles and stories about love and marriage, the position of women, how to bring up children, and lots of household hints. There were a number of more serious magazines and books too, about current events, literature, and social and philosophical questions. For the first time there were books written especially for children.

Most writers were men, but several women before Mary had broken the rules of their society and succeeded in being professional writers. A hundred years earlier there had been Aphra Benn, a romantic novelist and playwright. In Mary's own time, there was Catherine Macaulay, a historian; Mrs E. Johnson, who for eighteen years ran Britain's first Sunday newspaper; Anna Barbauld, a poet and writer of children's books; and a number of other women playwrights, poets, novelists and journalists. But these were the exceptions to the rule – inevitably, since few women received enough education even to write a clear letter.

Mary's first book was called *Thoughts on the Education of Daughters*. Mary identified more with the problems of adult women than of school-children. The most interesting parts of the book were those where she drew on her own experience of how hard it was for a

The title page of this magazine gives an idea of the range of subjects covered by women's magazines in Mary's time — beauty tips and fashion, cookery, music and literature, light news items, and politics.

Our studies were not extensive, nor very edifying. We learnt by rote either from the Dictionary, the Grammar, or Geography. Wrote no exercises, nor were we asked about our lessons.

From Elizabeth Ham, by herself.

LA BELLE ASSEMBLÉE,

OR

Bell's

COURT AND FASHIONABLE

MAGAZINE,

EMBELLISHMENTS.

1. Portrait of her Most Gracious Majesty Queen Charlotte.
2. Whole length Portrait of the Marchioness of Townshend, in her Court Dress.
3. Song, set to Music by Mr. Corri, expressly for this Work.
4. Three whole length Portraits, and four Head Dresses of the London Fashions.
5. Five whole length Portraits of Parisian Fashions.
6. Four New Patterns for Needle-Work.

33

woman to earn a living. She described the struggles of governesses, teachers, and other working women. She was the first writer to point out that all the injustices middle-class women suffered began with the fact that they could not work and earn money for themselves. Because women were dependent on men all their lives, men could get away with mistreating them. This was why it was vital that daughters should be educated.

A governess in Ireland

When this book was finished Mary had to look around for work yet again. The only job she could find was one she had always known she would hate – as a governess. She went to teach the eldest daughters of Lord and Lady Kingsborough, members of one of the richest and most aristocratic families in Ireland. Their home was Mitchelstown Castle, 160 kilometres south of Dublin.

It was a mixed experience. Mary was used to living in London, with lots of friends around her to exchange ideas with. She didn't like being stuck in the country, with few people to talk to. But to her surprise, Mary liked her pupils, and they liked her – partly because their mother didn't care about them very much. Mary also quite liked her employers, Lord and Lady Kingsborough, although she disapproved of their rich and spoiled way of life.

But Mary's character was not at all suited to being a governess. Governesses had a hard and lonely life. They had to live with the family that employed them, usually in the country and far away from their own friends and relatives. They had no life of their own. They were badly paid. The job also put them in an awkward social position. Most

The society of my father's house was not calculated to improve my good qualities or correct my faults; and almost the only person of superior merit with whom I had been intimate in my early days was an enthusiastic female who was my governess from fourteen to fifteen years old, for whom I felt an unbounded admiration because her mind appeared more noble and her understanding more cultivated than any other I had known.

Margaret Kingsborough's recollection of Mary Wollstonecraft

This illustration in Mary's book for children, Original Stories, *is by the poet and artist William Blake. Mary and William Blake became friends, for they had many ideas in common: both were horrified at the poverty and misery suffered by working people in Britain's cities.*

governesses, like Mary, were women from the professional middle class – no one else would have been educated enough. So a governess was socially above the servants. But she was below the family because she was their employee, if not quite their servant. Caught half-way between the two, she couldn't relax and be friends with either. It was like Mary's first job as a paid companion.

Mary couldn't accept that the Kingsboroughs would not treat her as their social equal. She felt that she was worth just as much as them – more, in fact, as she was not spoiled and idle as they were. Another

. . . am I to spend the rest of my life in this wretched bondage, forcibly suppressing my rage at the idleness, the apathy and the hyperbolical and most asinine stupidity of those fat-headed oafs, and on compulsion assuming an air of kindness, patience and assiduity?

Charlotte Brontë, on being a governess, 1836

difficult thing for Mary was that, like other servants, a governess was supposed to be quiet and polite all the time. She had to do what she was told, and keep her thoughts and feelings to herself. 'She must wear a cheerful face, or be dismissed.' Mary just couldn't do this. She was the kind of person who needs to express her feelings. If she was angry or depressed she couldn't force herself to smile sweetly and speak gently. It was largely because of this that she soon quarrelled with Lady Kingsborough and was dismissed from the job.

Mary hadn't wasted her time in Ireland. She had used her spare time to write a novel. Like most writers' first novels, it was really about herself, her own life and her own dreams. It was even called *Mary*. The main character was in many ways a picture of how Mary saw herself. 'Mary' was an intelligent woman surrounded by people who didn't understand her. But unlike the real Mary, the fictional Mary was rich and beautiful, and lots of men fell in love with her. The real Mary was not very successful in love.

'Old Maid's Petition'

This cruel cartoon shows how people often thought of unmarried women — as ugly, poor, and desperate for a man to marry. Mary wanted to prove, by her own life, that if a woman was allowed the chance to earn enough money herself, she could be comfortable and contented without a man to look after her.

Chapter Six

Revolution in the Air

Mary came back to London, and started
working full-time for Joseph Johnson, who
became one of her best and kindest friends.
He had plenty of work for her to do. She
tackled everything, from learned articles and
book reviews to children's stories.

Mary was now twenty-eight years old. For
the first time in her life she had regular work.
It was not well-paid, but just enough to keep
her going, and leave some over. This extra
money was spent on her family. Ned had
refused to be responsible for them and their
problems. Mary had to help her sisters and
her unsettled younger brothers, as well as her
now penniless father in Wales. She herself
lived a very simple life, with few clothes or
possessions.

One of her friends described her as 'a
philosophical sloven: her usual dress being a
habit of coarse cloth, such as is now worn by
milk-women, black worsted stockings, and a
beaver hat, with her hair hanging lank about
her shoulders' (Henry Fuseli). Mary was
never interested in clothes, but she had a
lively face, and her character and intelligence
won her plenty of friends. She had a good
social life. In a letter to Fanny's brother
George, she wrote: 'Whenever I am tired of
solitude I go to Mr Johnson's, and there I
meet the kind of company I find most
pleasure in.'

But still she was not happy. It was hard
being an unmarried woman. Not only
because of loneliness, but also because most

people despised single women. They thought that if a woman wasn't married it must be because no one would have her. And if a woman was clever and hard-working like Mary, instead of respecting her, people laughed and made cruel jokes about her.

Mary longed for someone to love. 'Without someone to love, the world is a desert to me,' she had written earlier. Several times she had met men she was interested in, but they did not fall in love with her. All too often, men expected women to be pretty and flirtatious and little more. Mary was different. She wanted to discuss serious subjects and be treated as an equal. She made most men feel uncomfortable.

Now she fell in love with an artist and writer from Switzerland, Henry Fuseli. He was a glamorous figure, famous, talented, and attractive. But Mary found nothing but unhappiness with him. At first he accepted her love, but he didn't really care for her, and besides he was already married. Even so, Mary found it hard to give him up.

The French Revolution
In other ways, however, the times were exciting for Mary, and for her Dissenter friends. They were optimistic that the new future they wanted for Britain was not far off. Their dream of a perfect society seemed to be coming true in America. Ten years earlier the people of America had won independence from Britain. They were determined to build their new country from the beginning as a land of justice, equality and happiness. Few white people in Mary's time recognised that in this so-called perfect society there were thousands of black slaves who certainly did not have equal rights. But white people in

America could think and say whatever they liked, and not be punished for it as the Dissenters were in England. Many people, including some Dissenters, were emigrating to America to join this new society of freedom and hope.

Closer to home, too, there were great political changes and hopes for a better future. The French Revolution had begun. The people of France overthrew their king and the upper class. They took control of the country and set up their own government. Their slogan was 'Liberty, Equality, Brotherhood'.

Radicals in England followed events in France keenly. They were sure the same thing would soon start to happen in Britain. One of Mary's friends, Dr Richard Price, said in a sermon in 1789, 'And now methinks I see the ardour for liberty catching and

America's Declaration of Independence from Britain, 4 July 1776. Britain fought to maintain its rule over the American colonies, but was finally defeated in 1782. Some people in Britain, especially radicals like Richard Price, had supported the Americans in their struggle for freedom.

spreading; a general amendment beginning in human affairs.'

But in fact the radicals' longing for revolution was not shared by most people in Britain. The government kept a close watch on the Dissenters, and tried to make sure their revolutionary ideas didn't catch on. Many working people too were afraid of change. They attacked Dissenters, looting their homes and setting fire to their books and papers. Mary was not afraid of attacks like this. She was one of the most enthusiastic supporters of the French Revolution. She was sure that when ordinary people started governing themselves, they

The French Revolution — The Storming of the Bastille. On 14 July 1789, crowds of the common people of Paris attacked and took over the Bastille prison. The Bastille was a hated symbol of the power of the king, so when it fell, the people were filled with excitement and confidence that their revolution would succeed. July 14th is still celebrated in France as a national holiday.

would end misery and injustice for ever.

These beliefs were expressed in *A Vindication of the Rights of Man*, published in 1790. A Vindication is an explanation, or argument in defence of something. This book put forward her view that everyone has the same rights. She wrote passionately about her sympathy for the poor and her contempt for the self-satisfaction of rich people who thought they were superior to everyone else. The result was an exciting book. Some people loved it, because it expressed exactly their own feelings. Others hated it. One way or another, lots of people read it and talked about it. At first it was published anonymously, but when the second edition was printed in 1791 it was attributed to Mary and she became a household name.

The Rights of Woman

At about the same time, a book called *Rights of Man* was published. It was by the well-known radical Tom Paine, and was widely read and discussed. Although she agreed with many of its political ideas, Mary felt that the book overlooked women, so partly in answer to it she decided to write another book. She called it *A Vindication of the Rights of Woman*. This is the book for which she is famous today. Mary began by saying that whenever she thought about the situation of women, 'the most melancholy emotions of sorrowful indignation . . . depressed [her] spirits'. It was true, she wrote, that most women were ignorant and seemed to be foolish, while even those who tried to help themselves found it hard to manage. But was this women's own fault? Did it prove that they were by nature inferior to men? No, Mary said.

[Women] must, from being treated like contemptible beings, become contemptible.

Mary Wollstonecraft in A Vindication of the Rights of Woman.

Mary was inspired by her own despair, anger and frustration at the position to which women were relegated in society. She was sympathetic to the difficulties working-class women faced; but most of her experience and her ideas about women's situation were drawn from the middle class, so she wrote mostly about their difficulties. In fact, she sometimes wrote as if the particular problems of middle-class women were common to all women.

She described how middle-class women were caught in a trap, which she believed had been set for them by men. Men had authority over women and took responsibility for them, and so women didn't need to look after themselves. Therefore they didn't 'need' education, or any opportunities to understand the world and develop their own abilities. Not surprisingly, their minds remained childlike and they filled their time with trivialities such as fashion and gossip. They became incapable of doing any responsible work outside the home or making useful contributions to society. The result was that they had no choice but to remain dependent on men. To add insult to injury, having denied them education men then complained about how empty-headed women were.

In addition, Mary said, men could never be satisfied, because they wanted women to be two different things – 'alluring mistresses' and 'rational mothers'. These two roles were contradictory; no woman could be both.

The first step towards solving the problem, Mary explained, was to end the legal subjugation of women. It was absolutely wrong for any human being to keep another in 'slavish obedience', as men kept women. If

[Even] Mary Wollstonecraft herself drew back at various points. Her ideas of sexual equality in education are limited to girls of her own estate and condition... Although she recognised theoretically that women must decide their own interests, in practice she appealed to men to release women from dependence.

Sheila Rowbotham, Hidden from History, *1973*

Men complain, and with reason, of the follies and caprices of our sex, when they do not keenly satirise our headstrong passions and grovelling vices. Behold, I should answer, the natural effect of ignorance!

Mary Wollstonecraft in A Vindication of the Rights of Woman.

they ended this injustice, men themselves would be better people. The second step was that men (and women too, who generally accepted the role men gave them) must accept that women were men's equals. Men must forget about wanting to have 'alluring mistresses' (who were only, after all, a kind of servant); and women must stop being flattered when men praised their beauty. Women must have equal education, equal opportunities and equal responsibilities. Then men would find that, instead of being 'contemptible beings', women became men's respected friends and partners.

One of Mary's ideas was so unusual that she hardly dared to mention it. It was that women should be allowed to vote for the government of the country. 'I may excite laughter,' Mary suggested, 'by dropping an hint . . . I really think that women ought to have representatives, instead of being arbitrarily governed without having any direct share allowed them in the deliberations of government.' Mary believed that all men should have the vote, and since women are men's equals, they should have it too. This idea seems perfectly natural to us now, but then it was thought ridiculous, particularly since at the time the only people who had the vote were the small number of rich landowners.

Shocking her ideas may have been, but Mary's book was a bestseller, and she became one of the most famous women in Europe. The reading public discussed Mary's theories eagerly. Some people must have read the book with excitement, feeling that here at last was someone who saw the truth and dared to tell it. Many, on the other hand, were put off by Mary's revolutionary politics, or hated her

How many women waste life away, the prey of discontent, who might have practised as physicians, regulated a farm, managed a shop?

Mary Wollstonecraft in A Vindication of the Rights of Woman.

'wild theory' of feminism. The writer Horace Walpole spoke for many people when he called Mary a 'philosophising serpent' and a 'hyena in petticoats'.

Unfortunately, even the people who were ready to accept the equality of women in theory, were not able to do much to put it into practice. They were a minority, without much influence. Even if they had had any power, the social revolution Mary was asking for would have taken years to bring about. Before the liberation of women could take place, a whole new set of laws and public institutions were needed. And before they could be achieved, public opinion had to support them – and that meant a transformation of people's private thoughts about women. It would be years before Britain was ready to begin the process.

Several thousand women marched from Paris to the royal palace of Versailles in October 1789. They were protesting against the shortage of food, and demanding that the king return to Paris and start negotiating with the parliament.

Chapter Seven

France

In France, the Revolution was not succeeding as easily as people had expected in the enthusiastic early days. There was a lot of violence and bloodshed. Some of its supporters in England began to wonder whether revolution was the best way for people to solve their problems, after all. Mary decided to go to France to see for herself what was happening. In a letter to her sister Everina, she was to call the Revolution 'the most extraordinary event that has ever been recorded'. She also hoped that the journey would help her forget her unhappy affair with Henry Fuseli. She went to Paris in December 1792 and joined the group of English radicals who were living there.

Her years in France brought great joys for Mary, and also great disappointments. She still believed firmly that ordinary people had the right to govern themselves. She was sure that a new age of peace and equality would begin soon. But at the same time, she was horrified at what was happening in Paris.

The people of France had formed a parliament, called the National Convention. At first, all its members had the same ideas about how to reform the country, but soon they started quarrelling among themselves. They divided into two parties, the Girondins, and the Montagne. The Girondins were rather like the Dissenters in England, and Mary made many friends among them. They believed in freedom, in the equality of men and women, and in solving problems without violence if possible.

The other party, the Montagne, was led by Robespierre, whom Mary hated. Their slogan was 'Revolution, One and Indivisible'. They represented the working people in France. Frustrated by many years of oppression and poverty, the masses were determined to abolish all distinctions between people and make everyone in France absolutely equal. They were even prepared to kill anyone who didn't agree with them. When the Montagne won power and the Girondins were expelled from the National Convention, the period known as 'The Terror' began.

And terrible it was. During the day there were festivals and celebrations to encourage the people to join together and work for a better future. But during the night, the secret police went from house to house arresting anyone the Montagne party thought was against them. Thousands of people were led to the guillotine to have their heads cut off.

An English view of the French Revolution, entitled with heavy sarcasm, 'A small supper, Parisian-style . . . a family of Sans-culottes refreshing after the fatigues of the day.' The 'Sans-culottes' were the militant revolutionaries of France (the name means 'Without Breeches' — they wore working men's trousers and not the breeches of the upper classes). The English cartoonist James Gillray, in a series of grotesque scenes like this, did a lot to turn public opinion in Britain against the French Revolution. Mary and her radical friends who supported the Revolution were only a small minority.

UNITÉ
INDIVISIBILITÉ
DE LA
RÉPUBLIQUE
LIBERTÉ
ÉGALITÉ
FRATERNITÉ

OU LA

MORT

*This French revolutionary slogan declares 'Unity and
Indivisibility of the Republic — Liberty, Equality, Brotherhood,
or Death.' On the left is a soldier of the defeated king, under a flag
saying 'The Terror of Kings'; on the right, a citizen of the new
republic wears the working man's trousers and soft cap that were
like a uniform of the revolution. His flag proclaims the 'Union of
Republicans.'*

The king was executed in January 1793, the queen a few months later. Many of Mary's Girondin friends were killed. The others had to go into hiding to escape arrest. Mary was filled with sorrow for them. She was sad too that progress for women seemed to have come to a brutal end – the Montagne did not believe in equality and freedom for women, and they executed women's leaders.

In spite of the bloodshed, Mary still believed that in the end the people would rule with peace and justice. They just needed more time to learn how to govern themselves. She wrote a book about the aims and dangers of revolution, called *A Historical and Moral view of the French Revolution*.

Falling in love

Even while she was witnessing all the horrors and violence and trying to understand why they were happening, Mary fell in love with an American man called Gilbert Imlay. He was a soldier, who had travelled a lot and written books about what he had seen. He was an attractive man, clever and entertaining. Mary thought he would treat her as an equal and respect her ideas. For a while she was happy. Her ideas about love were very romantic. She thought she had found the perfect man, and was sure he must love her as much as she loved him.

Before long, it became too dangerous to stay in Paris. Britain and France were at war, and all the British people in Paris were arrested, on suspicion of spying. (The British government wanted to defeat the French Revolution, to discourage the people in Britain from following the French example and rebelling.) Gilbert was safe because he was American, and Mary escaped

imprisonment by pretending she was his wife. Even so, they decided she must leave Paris.

Mary moved into a cottage near the deserted royal palace of Versailles. Here Gilbert came to visit her. In Paris at that time, it was not very unusual for couples to live together even though they were not married. People were looking for new ways of living as well as new ways of governing themselves. This suited Mary, who still did not believe in marriage. She thought people should be free. If two people truly loved each other, they would be faithful to each other whether they were married or not.

The price of freedom
But after a few months with Gilbert, Mary began to see that he did not love her as much as she wanted him to. He went away on long

'A victim of the Terror'
Manon Roland, a leading Girondin and one of Mary's friends in France, was arrested by the Montagne party in 1793. Here she is being led from prison to be tried for 'conspiring against the Revolution'. She was condemned, and sent to the guillotine to have her head cut off the same day.

business trips, and didn't answer her letters. She discovered that he was not perfect but just an ordinary man, and that his love for her did not mean more to him than anything else.

Little was known about contraception at that time, and soon Mary found that she was pregnant. She left her cottage and went to live with Gilbert in the port of Le Havre, where his business was. Her baby was born, and named Fanny after Mary's friend Fanny Blood. For a while Mary was very happy being a mother. But Gilbert left her and went to England. Not long afterwards Mary heard that he had another lover in London. She finally realised that she had been wrong about him, and that their relationship was over.

Mary was unhappy for a long time after this. All her life she had believed she would find perfect love. She thought she had found it with Gilbert. It was hard to admit to herself that she had been mistaken, and that the man she had chosen had betrayed her. Besides, now she had to face the hard consequences of freedom. Her man was free to leave and forget about her. But she had lost much of her freedom – she had an illegitimate daughter to bring up. How was she going to earn enough money?

Mary decided that she must return to England, where she would be able to go back to work for Joseph Johnson. It was a difficult decision to make. In spite of all the horrors she had seen, she still liked France better than England. She felt that French people respected each other more and had more understanding of justice than the English. She came back to London in April 1795, depressed and disappointed.

Although she never acknowledged it, [Mary] must have known that Imlay's desertion was perfectly in accord with their agreed theories about the importance of freedom and the immorality of maintaining a tie once feeling had ceased to sanction it.

Clare Tomalin, The Life and Death of Mary Wollstonecraft, 1974

Chapter Eight

Despair, Happiness, Death

There was little to make Mary happy when she got back to London. Her personal hopes had failed, and so had her political ones. She was miserable because Gilbert had abandoned her. Her friends didn't even sympathise with her much. They disapproved of the way she had behaved. London was much more conservative than revolutionary Paris. People did not accept the idea that women could be free to have affairs and have children without marrying.

The political atmosphere in London was very tense too. All hopes of a revolution had faded. The government refused to allow any change. It cracked down on all signs of rebellion and persecuted the Dissenters more than ever. (Joseph Johnson was fined and sentenced to nine months in prison, for selling a pamphlet criticising the government.) It was depressing for Mary to see that the new age she had believed in was not going to happen. Instead it seemed as though the old system of poverty, injustice and oppression would continue, perhaps for ever.

Mary sank into despair. In spite of having her baby Fanny to look after, she felt she had nothing to live for. Twice, she tried to kill herself. The first time, she took an overdose of the drug laudanum. Fortunately, friends found her and revived her. Even Gilbert tried to help. He suggested that for a change she should travel to Sweden and Norway to deal with some business for him. Mary always liked travelling, so she accepted this offer, and set off with Fanny and a nursemaid. It was a brave undertaking for a woman to make such a long journey without a male escort. She enjoyed the trip, and wrote lots of letters home describing the landscapes and the people of Scandinavia. Later these letters were published as a book.

Back in London, she was overcome by depression again and made a second attempt to commit suicide. This time, she jumped off Putney Bridge into the River Thames. A passing boatman saw her and pulled her out. Once more, she had to rally her energy and face life.

Love is a want of my heart . . . Aiming at tranquillity, I have almost destroyed all the energy of my soul . . . Despair, since the birth of my child, has rendered me stupid.

Mary, in a letter to Gilbert

Literary life in London

Gradually, things got better, in her personal life if not politically. She started working for Joseph again, and became popular among the intellectual and literary people of London. The greatest poets and writers of the time knew and liked her. Some of her new friends were women who, like her, had to struggle to earn their living, as actresses and writers. It was comforting to share stories of troubles with them.

Mary started to write another novel. Her aim was to put into it everything she knew about the unjust treatment of women. She wanted to share with others her experiences of love and disappointment, and what she had learned from them. The book was called *Maria, or The Wrongs of Woman*. It told the story of a rich woman unhappily married. Her husband locked her up and snatched away her child, wanting to get his hands on her money. The heroine escaped and travelled around the country, meeting many other women, who told her their terrible

'Mrs Thrale's breakfast table'
Mrs Thrale was a writer and a friend of Dr Samuel Johnson. Though the majority of artists and intellectuals were men, there were a few women, like Mrs Thrale and Mary, who became known as writers and were respected among intellectual circles in London.

stories. Many of them were poor women who had been seduced, betrayed, and abandoned. Their stories were dramatic but realistic, for they were based on the real experiences of people Mary knew or had heard of. It was unusual at the time for a writer to pay so much attention to humble and unfortunate people as Mary did in this book.

Mary spent a lot of time on this novel. She couldn't decide how it ought to end. She didn't want to make the heroine die. That would suggest that there was no hope for women. But it wouldn't be realistic to make the story end happily. She couldn't solve the problem, and never did finish it.

William Godwin

One of the people Mary got to know at this time was a famous philosopher, William Godwin. She had met him years before, and they hadn't liked each other. Now they had both changed, and they became good friends. They were both nervous about getting more involved – William because he was used to living by himself, Mary because she couldn't bear it if everything went wrong again, as it had with Gilbert.

But William was a very different person from Gilbert. He understood Mary and respected her, and shared her ideas about almost everything. Soon Mary decided she could trust him, and they became lovers. Perhaps Mary did not feel the same violent romantic passion for William that she had felt for Gilbert, but she was happy at last. She knew that, with all her faults, William loved her, and she felt a 'sublime tranquillity'.

They didn't want to be talked about, so they kept the relationship secret from their friends. They had to admit it, however, when Mary became pregnant. They thought it would be wrong for her to have another illegitimate child. The idea of freedom in love was good. But they both saw that in practice children were made to suffer a lot if their parents weren't married. So, although they both hated the idea of marriage, Mary and William were married in St Pancras Church on 29 March 1797.

Mary and little Fanny moved into William's house near St Pancras – William was fond of Fanny, and treated her like his own daughter. They settled down to a life of domestic happiness and hard work, and waited for the baby. Childbirth was extremely dangerous in those days. There were no

Portrait of Mary's husband William Godwin. William was a well-known philosopher. In his book Political Justice *he argued against strong central government. He thought there would be more justice and honesty if people formed small self-sufficient communities and governed themselves.*

antibiotics to prevent infections, and the mother or the child, or both, often died. Mary was not afraid, however, because she'd had an easy time when Fanny was born.

Mary's happiness was not destined to last long. Her labour began in the morning of 30 August, and her baby, another girl, was delivered that night. All seemed to be going well. But it was not. The placenta (the tissue which attaches the baby to the inside of the womb) had not come away. In the middle of the night, William sent for a doctor, who operated on Mary.

The result was a common one. The operation failed, and infection set in. There was no way of treating it. For ten days Mary fought for life, growing weaker and weaker from fever and loss of blood. She died on 10 September. She was only thirty-eight years old.

St Pancras' churchyard, where Mary was buried in 1797.

Chapter Nine

Neglected and Condemned

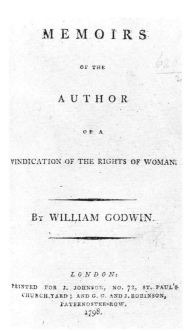

MEMOIRS

OF THE

AUTHOR

OF A

VINDICATION OF THE RIGHTS OF WOMAN.

By WILLIAM GODWIN.

LONDON:

PRINTED FOR J. JOHNSON, NO. 72, ST. PAUL'S CHURCH.YARD; AND G. G. AND J. ROBINSON, PATERNOSTER-ROW. 1798.

Title page of William Godwin's biography of Mary, which he started to write a few days after her death. He felt that Mary's character and life had been misunderstood, and he wanted to explain how unselfish and brave she was.

William was grief-stricken. 'I firmly believe there does not exist her equal in the world,' he wrote. Only two weeks after Mary's death, he began to write the story of her life. He wanted to show the world how good she had been, and how committed to justice. He supported all her ideas about social equality, marriage, and relationships, and he supported the unconventional things she had done to put her ideas into practice. If people knew about her, he thought, they would recognise that she spoke the truth. The position of women would begin to improve.

The opposite happened. For a few years Mary had been famous, and people had been excited by her books. But when the excitement died down, the position of women had not changed, and Mary's ideas were forgotten. Mary had argued against the image of women as weak and helpless. But in the century after her death, the Victorian era, people believed in this image even more than before. It became more difficult for any woman to challenge the stereotype, live independently and win respect for her work.

Mary's daughters did not try to carry on their mother's work. Fanny Imlay suffered from depression, and killed herself at the age of twenty-two. Mary Godwin (who married the poet Percy Bysshe Shelley) is famous now for something completely different – she created the story of the monster Frankenstein, which has inspired many film and television versions.

Would men but generously snap our chains, and be content with rational fellowship instead of slavish obedience, they would find us more observant daughters, more affectionate sisters, more faithful wives, more reasonable mothers – in a word, better citizens.

Mary Wollstonecraft in
A Vindication of the Rights of Woman.

Reaction against Mary's ideas

Why was Mary Wollstonecraft's work ignored? One reason was simply that she was too radical. People knew that Mary rejected marriage and much else that was traditional in British society. This alarmed them, and they didn't want to know any of her other ideas. There was, however, another reason. As the eighteenth century ended, the spirit of the times changed. Mary lived in the Age of Reason. It was a time of optimism. Many people in Europe and America believed that men and women could make themselves and their society perfect, if only they were given the chance to use their minds properly. Mary's ideas were part of this hopeful climate of opinion.

But events destroyed many of these hopes and dreams. The French Revolution produced, not a perfect society, but the military dictator Napoleon. In Britain too, there was a strong reaction against the Revolution. By the beginning of the nineteenth century, people couldn't think of words like 'equality' and 'brotherhood' without remembering the guillotine and all the violent events of the Revolution. This led them to distrust all revolutionary ideas and writings like Mary's.

This reversal of ideas affected the arts, as well as politics. The Age of Reason was followed by the Romantic era. Writers and artists came to believe that our instincts and emotions are stronger than our minds and our powers of reason. This dark and violent view of human nature had social effects. It was believed that most people would not be good unless their baser instincts were controlled by someone with authority over them. Governments must rule over the people, the rich over the poor, fathers over their families, men over women. These ideas were quite the opposite of Mary's.

The double standard

Most of all, Mary's ideas were neglected because people were more interested in her personal life. They condemned her for having had a lover and a child outside marriage, and decided that books written by a person like her couldn't be worth reading.

It is unlikely that a man would ever have been dismissed like this. Men and women were judged by different standards of morality. Men's love affairs were accepted without comment. A man's public actions were judged for themselves, not according to his private behaviour. But women were expected to be pure and innocent. Any woman who was not, was held to be worthless in every way. When people found something to criticise in a woman's behaviour, they dismissed her ideas as well, without even thinking about them.

Almost every time Mary was mentioned, she was condemned, even by women who were themselves demanding improvements in women's situation. A century later, Millicent Fawcett, for instance, fought for one of Mary's own ideas – that women should have the vote. But in the foreword to a new edition of Mary's *Vindication of the Rights of Woman* in 1891, she wrote of 'the errors of Mary Wollstonecraft's life', and said that when she read about them she was 'sickened for ever of the subject of irregular relations'. The same prejudices that made people neglect Mary's work, affected every feminist after her, especially in the Victorian era. Whenever a woman had new ideas or tried to

win new rights, people suspected that her personal life was unconventional too. They wanted to be able to say that any woman who drew attention to herself was wicked and worthless. That way, they would not have to respect her ideas either. In the face of such hostility, women who were trying to work for change were forced to make sure that their private lives were 'blameless'. Then they might, with difficulty, be able to convince people to take their ideas seriously.

The common image of women during the century after Mary's death. This sentimental picture shows a gentle, pretty, childlike woman, in the role most people thought women should be satisfied with — motherhood.

Women's progress in the 19th century.
In the second half of the nineteenth century, many brave women did force the world to listen. They succeeded in winning new opportunities and a better position for women. It was not easy: every gain was achieved only after a long struggle. By the end of the century, women had gained the right to education, including university education and medical training. New jobs had been opened up to them, particularly nursing and secretarial work. Marriage and divorce laws had been reformed, giving women more rights. They were on the way to winning the vote.

But in spite of all this progress, few people dared try to analyse the oppression of women from its basic causes, as Mary had done. To do that means investigating the fundamental relationship of men and women, and asking whether the sexes really do have different characters. And that, in the nineteenth century, was taboo. Women proved that they were as clever as men, as strong, and equally capable of leadership. But most people still believed that essentially women's nature was to be gentle, pure, beautiful – and dependent on men.

Mary argued that this image of women was false and oppressive. It has taken nearly two centuries for her idea to be widely accepted. And is her fight finished yet? Are women really equal to men now? For instance, do women earn the same wages as men? Is it as easy for a woman to reach the top of her profession as for a man? Have we stopped teaching girls that they should make themselves attractive? Mary Wollstonecraft would probably say that we still have a long way to go.

Women working as railway porters during the First World War. So many men were called up to join the army that women had to take over their jobs. It was women's chance to prove that they were capable of working just as well as men, and could be just as useful to their country. Because of the valuable work women did during the war, the government could no longer deny that they had a role to play in the nation's affairs and at last granted them the right to vote.

Do you not act [as tyrants] when you force all women, by denying them civil and political rights, to remain immured in their families groping in the dark?

Mary Wollstonecraft in
A Vindication of the Rights
of Woman.

TIME CHART

Events in Mary Wollstonecraft's life

1759 Mary Wollstonecraft born.
1763 Family move to Epping.
1765 Move to Barking, Essex.
1768 Move to Beverley, Yorkshire.
1774 Return to London.
1775 Mary meets Fanny Blood, at the home of some neighbours.
1776 Family move to Wales.
1777 Return to London.
1778 Mary works as a companion to Mrs Dawson.
1782 Mary's mother dies. Her sister Eliza marries. Mary goes to live with Fanny Blood's family.
1783 Mary goes to look after Eliza, persuades her to leave her husband. They open a school in Newington Green.
1785 In February, Fanny goes to marry her fiancé in Lisbon. Mary joins her in November. Fanny dies in childbirth.
1786 The school closes. Mary writes *Thoughts on the Education of Daughters*, and takes a job as governess with Lord and Lady Kingsborough in Ireland.
1787 Mary is dismissed, returns to London.
1788 Mary meets Henry Fuseli. Joseph Johnson publishes *Mary* and *Original Stories*.
1790 *A Vindication of the Rights of Man* published.
1791 Second edition of Mary's *Vindication* published.
1792 Publication of *A Vindication of the Rights of Woman*. Mary goes to Paris.
1793 Mary meets Gilbert Imlay. Moves out of Paris, becomes pregnant.
1794 Mary moves to Le Havre, Fanny is born. *A Historical and Moral View of the Origin and Progress of the French Revolution* published.
1795 Return to London. Attempts suicide. Journey in Scandinavia, followed by another suicide attempt.
1796 *Letters written during a Short Residence in Sweden, Norway and Denmark*. Forms relationship with William Godwin. Becomes pregnant.
1797 Marries William. Baby Mary born, and Mary Wollstonecraft dies on 10 September.

Key dates (1694 - 1979)

1694 Mary Astell's *A Serious Proposal to the Ladies* published.

1776 American Independence.

1789 Beginning of the French Revolution.

1793 The French king executed.

1847 Queen's College for Women opened, mostly to train governesses.

1850 First Girls' Public Day School opened.

1854 Crimean War. Florence Nightingale's organisation of army hospital helps open up nursing as an acceptable profession for women.

1857 Matrimonal Causes Act: a deserted wife can keep her earnings.

1860 The Society for Promoting the Employment of Women founded.

1863 Girls allowed to take the Cambridge Examinations (equivalent to A-level).

1866 First petition for female suffrage presented to parliament.

1869 First women's university college founded at Hitchin, later to become Girton, Cambridge.

1870 Married Women's Property Act – women living with their husbands can keep their earnings.
Education Act – all local authorities to provide schools.

1875 Law allowing universities to grant degrees to women.

1882 Married Women's Property Act – married women can own property.

1888 Women allowed to vote in local elections.

1895 Royal College of Surgeons accepts women members.

1897 National Union of Women's Suffrage Societies founded.

1914-19 First World War – new employment opportunities for women.

1918 Men over 21 and women householders over 30 granted the vote. Women over 21 can become MPs.

1919 First woman MP, Nancy Astor.
Sex Disqualification Removal Act – women can become magistrates, jurors, barristers, and solicitors.

1928 Women get the vote on the same terms as men.

1929 The first woman cabinet minister, Margaret Bondfield.

1970 Equal Pay Act – men and women must receive the same pay for the same job.

1975 Sex Discrimination Act.

1979 Margaret Thatcher first woman Prime Minister.

Index

Further Reading
The Life and Death of Mary Wollstonecraft Claire Tomalin (Penguin)
Mary Wollstonecraft: A Critical Study Ralph Wardle (Bison Books)
The Changing Status of Women Olivia Bennett (Bell & Unwin)

The publishers wish to thank the following for supplying
photographs for this book:

British Library pages 13, 35, 56; British Museum pages 2, 23, 29,
30, 31, 55; Mansell Collection cover (below), pages 9, 11, 14, 16,
20, 33, 36, 39, 40, 44, 46, 47; Mary Evans Picture Library cover
(top), pages 6, 15, 18, 21, 24, 27, 39, 40, 49, 53, 59, 61; National
Portrait Gallery page 54.